World Series Champions: Washington Nationals

Outfielder José Guillén

Outfielder Lane Thomas

WORLD SERIES CHAMPIONS

WASHINGTON NATIONALS

JOE TISCHLER

CREATIVE EDUCATION / CREATIVE PAPERBACKS

CREATIVE SPORTS

Published by Creative Education and Creative Paperbacks
P.O. Box 227, Mankato, Minnesota 56002
Creative Education and Creative Paperbacks are imprints of
The Creative Company
www.thecreativecompany.us

Art Direction by Tom Morgan
Book production by Ciara Beitlich
Edited by Jill Kalz

Photographs by Alamy (Christopher Szagola/CSM), Corbis (Rich
Pilling, Robert Riger), Getty (Bettmann, Rob Carr, Focus on Sport,
Icon Sportswire, Mitchell Layton, Jim McIsaac, Don Smith, Rob
Tringali/Stringer, The Washington Post)

Library of Congress Cataloging-in-Publication Data
Names: Tischler, Joe, author.
Title: Washington Nationals / Joe Tischler.
Description: Mankato, MN : Creative Education and Creative
    Paperbacks, [2024] | Series: Creative sports. World Series
    champions | Includes index. | Audience: Ages 7-10 | Audience:
    Grades 2-3 | Summary: "Elementary-level text and engaging sports
    photos highlight the Washington Nationals' MLB World Series win,
    plus sensational players associated with the professional baseball
    team such as Dennis Martinez."-- Provided by publisher.
Identifiers: LCCN 2023011824 (print) | LCCN 2023011825 (ebook)
    | ISBN 9781640268371 (library binding) | ISBN 9781682773871
    (paperback) | ISBN 9781640269903 (pdf)
Subjects: LCSH: Washington Nationals (Baseball team)--History--
    Juvenile literature. | World Series (Baseball)--History--Juvenile
    literature.
Classification: LCC GV875.W27 T57 2024 (print) | LCC GV875.W27
    (ebook) | DDC 796.357/6409753--dc23/eng/20220314
LC record available at https://lccn.loc.gov/2023011824
LC ebook record available at https://lccn.loc.gov/2023011825

Printed in China

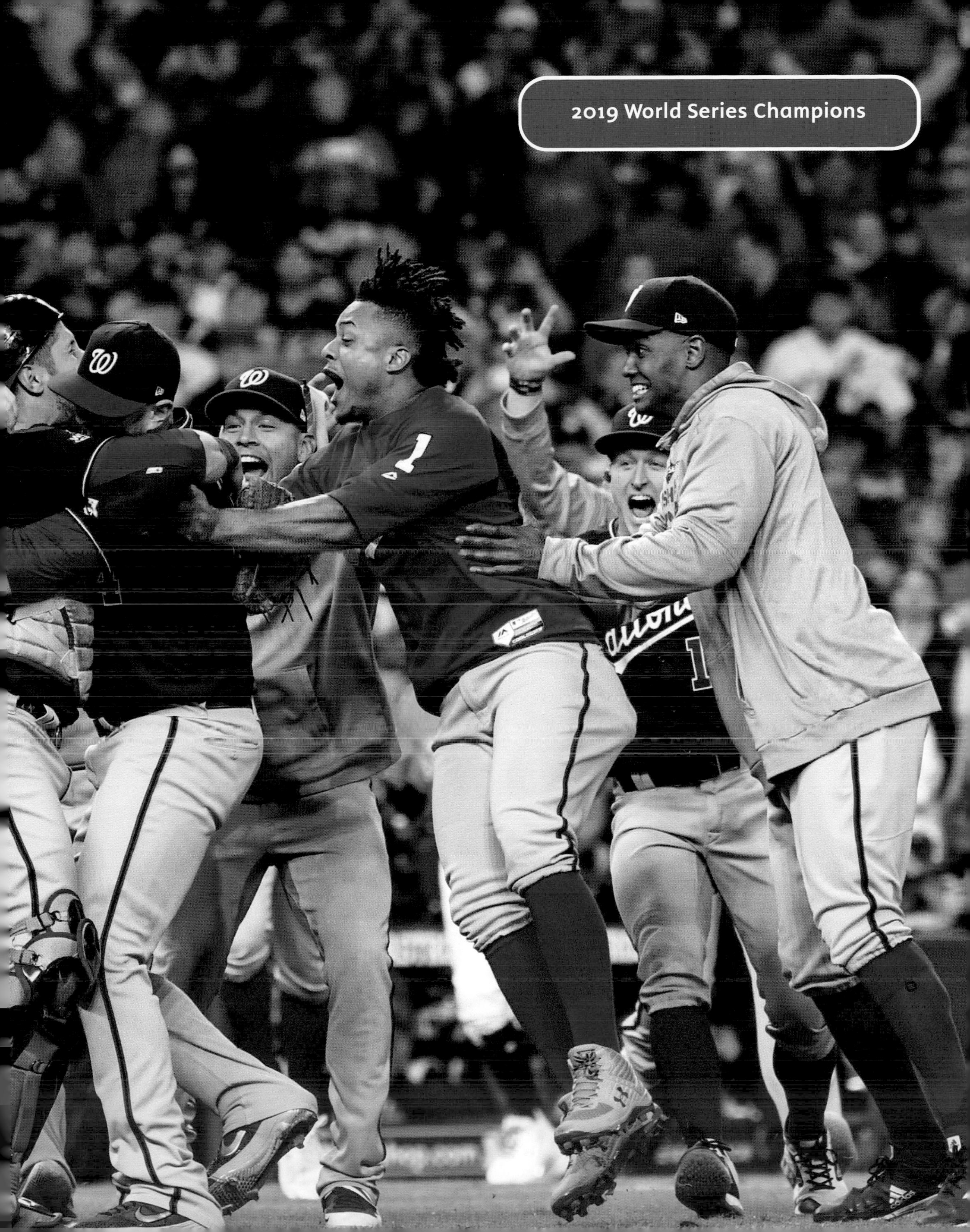

2019 World Series Champions

Outfielder Juan Soto

CONTENTS

Home of the Nationals

ashington, D.C., is the capital of the United States. The nation's president lives there. The Nationals baseball team plays there, too. Fans love to go to a **stadium** called Nationals Park to cheer them on.

The Washington Nationals are a Major League Baseball (MLB) team. They are part of the National League (NL) East Division. Their biggest **rivals** are the Philadelphia Phillies. All MLB teams try to win the World Series to become champions.

Pitcher Pedro Martínez

Naming the Nationals

ashington, D.C., has been home to many professional baseball teams. The Washington Senators played in the American League from 1901 to 1960. For most of that time, they were also called the Nationals. When baseball returned to the area in 2005, the team chose "Nationals" as its name.

Outfielder Andre Dawson

Nationals History

Today's Nationals were formed in 1969 in Montreal, Canada. There they were called the Expos. Montreal didn't make its first **playoff** appearance until 1981. Three Baseball **Hall of Fame** members were on that team. Andre Dawson and Tim Raines manned the outfield. Catcher Gary Carter won hitting and fielding awards. The Expos fell just shy of reaching the World Series.

The Expos continued to play good ball. But they couldn't make it back to the playoffs. Third baseman Tim Wallach played in five All-Star games. He won multiple Gold Glove and Silver Slugger Awards. The best fielders and hitters get them.

The Expos moved to Washington, D.C., in 2005. They became the Nationals. They weren't very good. Twice they lost more than 100 games in a season. The team started winning in 2012. They made the playoffs for the first time in more than 40 years. Outfielder Bryce Harper was a star. He was named NL **Rookie** of the Year. Three years later, he was named NL Most Valuable Player (MVP).

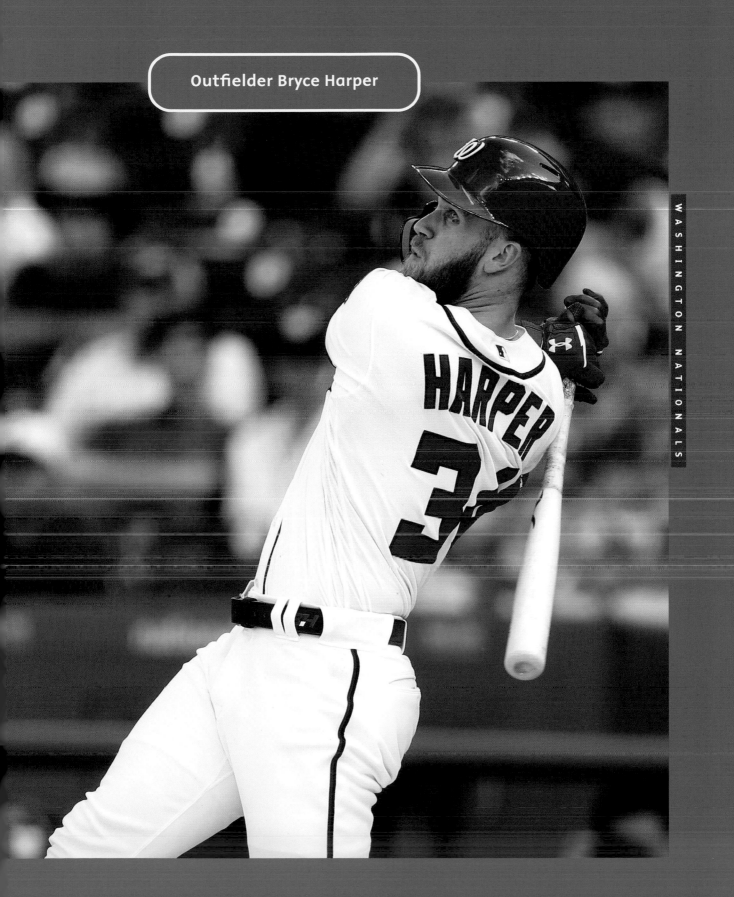

Outfielder Bryce Harper

The Nationals won their first playoff series in 2019. Max Scherzer and Stephen Strasburg were two of baseball's best pitchers. Outfielder Juan Soto belted home runs. These players boosted the Nationals to their first World Series. They beat the Houston Astros to win their first championship!

Other Nationals Stars

Many stars have played for the Nationals. Steve Rogers and Dennis Martínez were great pitchers. Martínez once threw a **perfect game**.

Vladimir Guerrero threw out base runners from right field. Pedro Martínez struck out batter after batter.

Outfielder Vladimir Guerrero

Outfielder Victor Robles

Victor Robles and Lane Thomas are rising, young hitters. Fans hope they can help bring the Nationals another championship soon!

About the Nationals

Started playing: 1969

. . . .

League/division: National
  League, East Division

. . . .

Team colors: red, white, and blue

. . . .

Home stadium: Nationals Park

. . . .

WORLD SERIES CHAMPIONSHIPS:

  2019, 4 games to 3 over Houston Astros

. . . .

Washington Nationals website:
  www.mlb.com/nationals

. . . .

Glossary

Hall of Fame—a museum in which the best players of all time are honored

perfect game—a game where a pitcher doesn't allow a runner on base the whole game

playoff—games that the best teams play after a regular season to see who the champion will be

rival—a team that plays extra hard against another team

rookie—a first-year player

stadium—a building with tiers of seats for spectators

Outfielder Tim Raines

Index